Managing the Union Shop

Phillip B. Wilson
President, Labor Relations Institute

> TO ORDER ADDITIONAL COPIES
>
> To inquire about single or quantity orders of
>
> ## *Managing the Union Shop*
>
> Email us at sales@LRIonline.com

VISIT US ONLINE http://LRIonline.com

Copyright ©2016 by Labor Relations Institute. All rights reserved.

No part of this book may be reproduced or transmitted in any form and by any means without prior written permission of the publisher, except in the case of brief quotations in book reviews and critical articles.

Published by Labor Relations Institute.

SECOND EDITION

Printed in the United States of America.

ISBN: 1505222753
ISBN-13: 978-1505222753

Table of Contents

Managing the Union Shop 5
What's the Deal with This Book? 5
Administering the Union Contract—The Manager's Role 6
Manager's Roles 7
How a Union Changes Your Job 10
The Union's Role 11
Sample Management Rights Clause 12
An Example 13
Why the Contract Isn't Always Right 14
Facts of Life in a Unionized Environment 15
Characteristics of a Strong Leader in a Union Shop 16
Unfair Labor Practices 18
Know the Contract 20

The Grievance Process 22
What's a Grievance? 22
Typical Grievance Procedure 23
Sample Grievance Procedure 27
Responding to Grievances 31
Best Defenses for Grievances 32
What to Do When a Grievance Is Filed 34

Just Cause 37
What is Just Cause? 37
Comparison to "At-Will" Employment 37
The Three Tests for "Just Cause" 38
Factors Used to Determine Just Cause 39
Creating a Good Record 43
The Role of Seniority 44
Combining Offenses 44

The "12-month" Rule of Thumb 45
Accelerating Offenses 46
How to Write a Defensible Written Reprimand 47
Sample Written Reprimand 48
Communication—Witnesses 49

Past Practice and Erosion 51
Management Rights in the "State of Nature" 51
An Example of Erosion 52
No "Gifts" 53
Grievance Settlements and Erosion 53
Why You Are Most Likely to Erode Your Contract 54
Past Practice 54
Where Does Past Practice Come From? 55
Uncommon Occurrences and Equivocal Actions 56
The Problem with Past Practice 57
How Past Practice Comes Up in Grievances 58
"Fixed and Established" Past Practice 58
Using the Grievance Record to Evaluate Past Practice 60
How A Company Can Overcome Past Practice 62

Leading in a Union Shop 67
The Connection Model: The Three Pillars of Approachable Leadership 69
TOOL: Recognizing Approachability Gaps 70
The Case for Approachability 73
Approachability is Teachable 75

Conclusion 77
Notes 78

About the Author 85
About Labor Relations Institute, Inc. 86

INTRODUCTION
Managing the Union Shop

As a manager or supervisor in a unionized company, you have a unique job. Besides your daily responsibilities, you also must know about unions and basic labor law. You can be the best manager in the world. However, without a solid knowledge of the rules and responsibilities in a union shop you can get yourself—and your company—into a lot of trouble. That is the purpose of this book. To give you the background you need to be an effective manager in a unionized environment.

This book walks you through some of the major things you need to know about unions to be a good manager or supervisor. By the way, from now on I will refer to management or supervisory employees as "managers." No matter your actual title, you share one job. You manage labor relations in a way that lets your company meet its goals with little trouble from the union.

What's the Deal with This Book?

You'll notice that this isn't like most books you have seen on how to be a good manager. It works like a labor contract! For years, most contracts were small books. Some were even designed to fit in a union steward's shirt pocket. Why? Not just to make it hard to read—although sometimes the fine print can be tough to decipher. No, the reason it is small is so it is portable. Stewards want the contract with them always, in case they need it to dispute something that pops up.

We've designed this book the same way—while it may not fit in your shirt pocket, it is small and handy. It even has some blank pages in the back so you can use it to take notes. The idea is not for you to read this once and then thrown in a desk, never to see the light of day. It is a book you can <u>use</u>.

Administering the Union Contract—The Manager's Role

Maybe you already have experience managing in a unionized environment. You'll still pick up tips that help you do a better job and understand how your role fits into the labor relations big picture. But most people these days have had no experience with unions. You have more to learn, and you may want to review this book more than once. Some of the items we will cover include:

- How your job changes in a unionized environment
- The union's "reactionary" role, including grievances and arbitration procedures
- Union "facts of life"
- Avoiding unfair labor practices
- The importance of knowing the contract

Later we will look at the grievance and arbitration process. You will learn more about "just cause" provisions common to many labor contracts. You will also learn about past practice, and how your daily management decisions can have a significant impact on the ability to manage the company.

Manager's Roles

First, it's critical to understand your role in administering the union contract. The manager's role is an important one. As in a non-union organization, you're responsible for the day-to-day management issues that come up during regular production. You make work assignments, you respond to quality issues, handle questions about policy or procedure, plus any number of other problems.

1. Administer the Contract

Once a union contract goes into effect, you also become responsible for the day-to-day administration of the contract's provisions. As a manager, you must know the labor contract inside out. You will be expected to follow the various provisions as they relate to things like job bidding, job assignment, overtime assignment, enforcement of work rules, and other issues. Frequently the union is represented in the workforce by a shop steward—sometimes more than one steward—whose job is to watch managers and make sure they follow the contract. If they feel you ignored the labor agreement they can object, usually through a grievance procedure.

As a manager, it is important that you also carefully follow the labor contract. We will learn more about this later. For now, remember that failure to follow the agreement can lead either to grievances on the one hand or "erosion" of management's authority on the other. Unless part of the company strategy, it is essential that you follow the labor contract as closely as possible.

2. Intermediary

In addition to administering the contract, the manager also plays a critical "intermediary" role. You must enforce contract provisions in a way that is consistent with management's view of the agreement while dealing with the objections and grievances of union stewards and other union officials. Your effectiveness in this intermediary role determines whether the union files grievances. It will also dictate the type of relationship you have with the union.

There are two aspects to this intermediary role. At first, you will relay information to management, particularly regarding potential contract issues. Pretend for a minute that the way you assign overtime under a new labor contract is different than under the old contract. Employees accustomed to the old system may object, and may not fully understand its provisions. As part of your intermediary role, you might notify your human resources manager or plant manager about the apparent misunderstanding of the new rules. Several things could happen next.

Your manager may decide to approach the union's leadership to explain the misunderstanding and ask for their help in clarifying the issue for members. Management may choose to do nothing and tell you to continue enforcing the new contract provisions. Alternatively, you may be asked to bend the rules and give in to the requests of union members, even though this does not strictly comply with the labor contract. Why would management do this? Well, if the company did not like the new contract provision, it might want to create more suitable "past practice" to use in the future. We'll go into this further later.

The important thing to understand right now is that management has no opportunity to decide how it wants to approach the problem if it is not aware of the dispute in the first place. That's why your role as an intermediary is critical to the company's labor relations strategy.

The second important part of your intermediary role is to calm misunderstandings in the workforce. You must communicate management's position on various issues. In some ways, this job becomes easier in a unionized environment because you can expect employees to rely on their union for information about day-to-day work-related matters. However, unions will periodically try to create misunderstandings or issues for their purposes. In these situations, your role is more like that of a mediator, attempting to calm disputes and trying to make sure employees don't lose sight of the company's goal.

3. Follow the Company Policies
Also, you remain responsible for following the regular company procedures and policies that are not altered by the labor agreement. Company work rules, quality rules, and other regulations typically remain in place even after a union contract goes into effect. Finally, you must balance the production needs of the organization with whatever limits the labor contract imposes.

How a Union Changes Your Job

A union contract changes your job in different ways. In some ways, the job becomes easier. Your role in a unionized environment becomes more that of an administrator. You will spend a lot of your time administering contract rules agreed upon in advance by the company and the union. In some cases, this means less need to explain management decisions, particularly when you are merely implementing the union contract. Many times, when employees would usually complain to management, you can direct them to their union officials who share responsibility for the provisions of the contract.

However, in other ways, your job can be more frustrating. If you normally have much discretion or make changes "on the fly," you may find a union labor agreement restrictive. This, of course, will depend on the exact language of your contract agreement. While management will reserve certain rights for managers, you will lose discretion in any area where there is a specific contract provision that dictates how the labor agreement deals with that issue.

In your role of contract administrator, you must carefully follow the provisions of the contract. If you fail to follow the contract this often causes grievances. It can also set a precedent for the company, which could lead to contract erosion or bad past practice, both of which the union will use against the company in future grievances.

The Union's Role

What part does the union play in a unionized environment? The union's role is primarily "reactionary." In other words, management initiates most actions in the workplace, and the union has the right to protest or appeal those actions if it believes they are in violation of the contract agreement.

Here is a quote from a shop steward's manual regarding the role of the steward in reacting to management:

> "The problems of management are not your problem. It is not up to you to make the workers toe the line or to increase efficiency. That's the bosses' worry. Your job is to protect the workers and to get their grievances settled quickly and satisfactorily."

Generally, the union cannot protest management's right to act or to initiate action. This is distinct from the union opposing the effects of management's actions. Of course, this assumes that the contract does not control an issue. If a contract said, for example, that management gives up its right to assign work tasks to employees and instead gives that right to the union, then the union could protest if a manager attempted to assign work to an employee. Most of the time management will not agree to such broad prohibitions.

Most contracts give management the right to act but establish parameters regarding how to exercise that power. Let's pretend that instead of the broad provision I just described, the company and union agree that although management has the right to make work assignments, it may only make those assignments based on seniority. In that case, management preserves its right to assign work but agrees to restrictions on how to exercise that right. This is how union contract provisions typically work.

Except in life or death safety matters, most union stewards will tell a member who disagrees with a management decision to "work now, grieve later." This is important to remember. If you face an employee who is considering whether to refuse a request, it's a good idea to encourage them to "work now, grieve later." Union stewards will usually rely on the grievance procedure in situations where they feel the employer has failed to follow the contract.

Most contracts contain what is called a Management Rights clause. This says that management retains the right to act unless that right is explicitly given up in the agreement. See if you can find a clause like that in your contract.

Sample Management Rights Clause

Section 1
The management of its employees, the control of the premises, and the direction of the work force are vested exclusively with the Company and include, but are not limited to the following: the direction of the work force which includes the right to hire, assign, promote, demote, terminate, or transfer employees; to discharge, suspend, or otherwise discipline; to require overtime to work and assign to such work those employees deemed by it most capable; to determine, establish, or modify staffing requirements, job duties, workload, or quality of workmanship for all classifications; to set standards of

efficiency; to relieve employees from duty because of lack of work; to subcontract any work deemed advisable; to promulgate and enforce conduct and working rules and impose penalties for violations thereof; to reduce operations; to plan, direct, change, schedule, and control the operations of the Company and the personnel, methods, equipment, and machinery used in the operation of the Company; to transfer or cease any or all operations of its facility; and to determine the number of hours per day or per week operations shall be carried on. Such rights shall be exclusive to the Company.

Section 2
The parties further understand and agree that all inherent common law management functions and prerogatives which the Company has not waived in this Agreement are retained and vested exclusively in the Company.

The bottom line is that managers act to keep the administrative right to manage, while the union works to limit that right based on the language in the collective bargaining agreement. For this reason, it is essential that you not defer to the union when deciding whether to act. Failure to act when the right exists can lead to potential constraints on management's actions in the future.

An Example

Let's imagine that your contract has a provision that says management will try to give 24-hour notice of overtime, but that this is not required. What would you do if one day there was an emergency and you needed to have someone work overtime, but couldn't give any notice? Assume the employee objects, shows you the contract provision, and points out that even though the provision says management does not always have to give notice, in practice it always does. To complicate things a little more, let's also assume that you know you could give 24-hour notice today and still get the work completed tomorrow if you had to. What would you do?

If you said you would require the employee to work the overtime anyway, you are on the right track. Even if the employee complains to a union steward and threatens a grievance, you should hold your ground. Tell the steward and the worker to "work now, grieve later." Why? Well, if you backed down, the union could argue that your action shows a change in management's practice—the notice provision has become required and is no longer optional. The union will use your actions as proof that the terms of the agreement have changed through the parties' actions.

Why the Contract Isn't Always Right

When managers first start working in a unionized environment, this is often confusing. They think the wording of the contract will determine the outcome of any grievances. While this is usually the case, it certainly is not always. There are many situations where the actions of after the parties *sign* the agreement become more important in interpreting the work rules than the contract itself. For this reason, it is important that managers not only follow the contract but also act to protect the rights of management.

Facts of Life in a Unionized Environment

Managers in unionized companies must get used to certain "facts of life." First, hostility toward the union is usually self-defeating. The union is the exclusive bargaining agent for all employees in the bargaining unit. You cannot deal directly with employees on their wages, hours, or conditions of employment.

Hostility on your part normally just results in headaches above and beyond those you typically find in the administration of the labor contract. Make no mistake; there are times when the union may try to instigate hostility as a strategy. This can occur at the bargaining table or against a manager with whom the union, for some reason, has a problem. If you are ever in a situation like this, the best approach is to be a strong leader (see Chapter 5 for some great tips).

Characteristics of a Strong Leader in a Union Shop

Strong leaders earn the respect of the union by being fair, firm, credible, consistent, and predictable. Always try to treat employees fairly but within the rules of the contract. Don't bend to pressure to make exceptions to the contract. Over time, you will become known as a credible leader. The union may not always agree with what you do, but it will know where you stand. This helps the union deal with its members, who may not always be reasonable either.

It's important to be open with the union's leadership and to try not to surprise them; it is equally important not to diminish the rights given to management. Do not attempt to negotiate with a union steward over an issue that is within the rights of management. Instead, explain the decision and emphasize that it is within the rights of management. If the union disagrees, it can appeal through the grievance process. The point is not to be confrontational. Let the union know you will abide by the terms of the contract where they apply. Otherwise, you will firmly enforce management's right to manage.

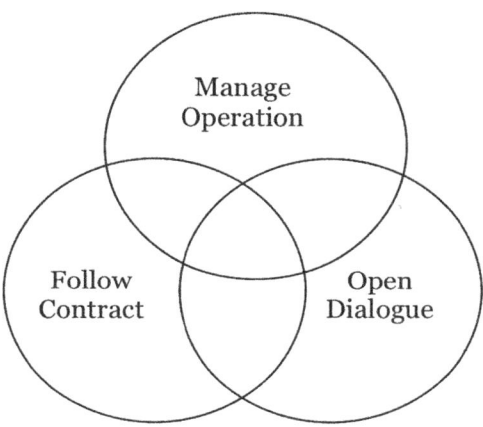

Another thing to remember about the "facts of life" in a unionized environment is that nice guys finish last. Attempts to bend the rules to help someone because you feel sorry for them will inevitably come back to bite you. Never forget that the steward's job is to follow the contract to the letter.

Sometimes a steward, or someone else in a position of power in the union, may ask for special treatment outside of the bounds of the contract. Deny this, even if there's the threat of a grievance. If you follow the terms of the contract, you will always be on firm ground should there be a grievance or arbitration. Any exceptions in the contract can become grounds for an objection, or worse yet, become the basis for past practice. In future contract negotiations, this can erode management's authority to manage.

Unfair Labor Practices

Another important role of a manager in a unionized environment is to avoid committing unfair labor practices (ULP for short). Unions sometimes file ULP charges during the term of the contract or especially during labor contract negotiations. There are three common areas for charges against employers in the unionized environment:

1. **Unilateral Changes:** The most common unfair labor practice charge filed against a manager is typically for a unilateral change in working conditions and a failure to bargain. Once a union is voted in, a company is legally required to bargain over all wages, hours, and conditions of employment for members of the bargaining unit. Managers are not allowed to negotiate individual terms or conditions of employment for employees in the unit.

   Often a union will look at a manager's actions, particularly something that is favorable for one group of employees at the expense of others. They will claim the change is a unilateral change of working conditions. Because management did not bargain with the Union over the modification, that is an unfair labor practice.

   The best way to avoid charges—even when the "change" you've made is something that you believe to be within the management rights clause of the contract—is to notify the union of the modification. If the union does not ask to bargain over the proposed change, after 60 days it will have waived its unfair labor practice claim. Of course, the union may choose to negotiate. In this case, the company must decide whether it wishes to engage in bargaining or make the argument that the change is not a required subject for bargaining. This is a decision that is typically made by a manager above you.

2. **Discrimination:** Another unfair labor practice charge that managers must avoid is unlawful discrimination. It is illegal to act against an employee due to his or her support of the union. To prevent unfair labor practices for discrimination, it's important that managers follow the TIPS rule—TIPS is an acronym for:
    a. Threats
    b. Interrogation
    c. Promises
    d. Surveillance

   An employer and its agents, including managers, may not threaten, interrogate, promise or engage in surveillance of employees in the bargaining unit, where the purpose of that action is to discriminate against someone's union membership or sympathies. These charges are less common in a unionized environment, but always follow the TIPS rule.

3. **Domination:** "Employer domination" of the union is a more common charge against managers. This rule was established in the 1940s, long before teams became so important for successful American companies. The law states that a company may not assist or provide support to the union. The National

Labor Relations Board has interpreted the term "union" not just to include labor organizations, like a union local, but also employee teams and committees.

To avoid a charge of "employer domination," be sure that no employee team or committee engages in "bargaining" over wages, hours, or conditions of employment. For example, if employees make suggestions and management then comes back with counter-suggestions—especially if management can "reject" the ideas offered by employees—this can be considered unlawful negotiating.

The National Labor Relations Board has approved employee teams or committees where they the union approves them, or if the team is given management authority over an area without excessive review by management. A rule of thumb is to notify the company of any committee or team that you plan to use to resolve a workplace issue. Be sure that the union labor contract authorizes the committee or team.

Know the Contract

The final role of the manager in a union setting is to know the contract. You will avoid many potential problems if you do. Understand, for example, what are the most grieved contract provisions. You should also know what are management's best defenses to grievances. Be sure the contract is applied continuously and consistently. Finally, adhere to past practice; this protects management's authority and ability to act in the future.

That covers the basic roles of a supervisor or manager in a unionized workplace. Simply going through the process of handling grievances, and occasionally even arbitrations, will help teach you more. Keep in mind the roles you play as a manager, and you will effectively manage responsibilities in this new unionized environment.

CHAPTER 2
The Grievance Process

Managers in a union shop must understand both grievance procedures and the concept of just cause. Below you will find examples of the typical grievance procedure, how to defend against grievances, and some tips on avoiding grievances. It will also thoroughly explain the concept of "just cause."

What's a Grievance?

For our purposes, a grievance is a formal complaint raised by an employee. The dispute resolution process is called a grievance procedure. Almost all labor contracts have some grievance procedure. If you currently have a labor contract, it will help to have a copy of that while you view this. A typical grievance form might look like the one on the next page:

Widget Workers, Local 007 Grievance Form			
Employee Name:		Employee #	
Department:		Classification:	
Supervisor:		Shift:	
Describe the facts giving rise to the grievance.			
What contract provision was violated?			
What relief is requested?			
Decision of immediate supervisor:			
Supervisor signature:		Date:	
Employee signature:		Date:	
Union steward:		Date:	
To enforce contract time limits, date stamp grievance upon receipt.			

Typical Grievance Procedure

A grievance procedure is a multi-step process that reviews complaints about contract violations. At each step in the process, the grievance is either resolved or appealed to the next step. A typical procedure might require the employee to first file a grievance with his or her immediate manager, usually in the presence of the local union steward. The manager, the steward, and the employee try to resolve the grievance. If they can't resolve it, the employee and the union have the right to take the grievance to the next level.

The second step might be an appeal to a department manager. If the employee, the union, and the department manager cannot come to a resolution, then the grievance is appealed to the next level. Usually the human resources manager.

If the grievance still isn't resolved, the employee and union might appeal next to the plant manager. This is the fourth step. If the grievance is still not resolved at the last step, most procedures provide for binding arbitration. An outside arbitrator, often a lawyer or other labor expert, will act as a judge over the grievance.

The arbitrator conducts a hearing, which is a kind of "mini-trial." Each side presents its witnesses and documents to either prove or defend against the grievance. When the arbitrator has all the evidence, a decision is reached based on the facts and the law. The arbitrator looks at things like the wording of the contract, the past practices of the company, and the way other companies made similar decisions.

In termination cases, one of the important concepts an arbitrator relies on is "just cause," which we'll discuss a little later. The decision of an arbitrator is typically final and binding on all parties.

Now you can understand why an important part of your job is to administer the union contract such that if the union takes a grievance to arbitration, the independent arbitrator will rule for the company.

The flow chart on the following page summarizes the typical grievance process. After that, you can review a sample grievance procedure.

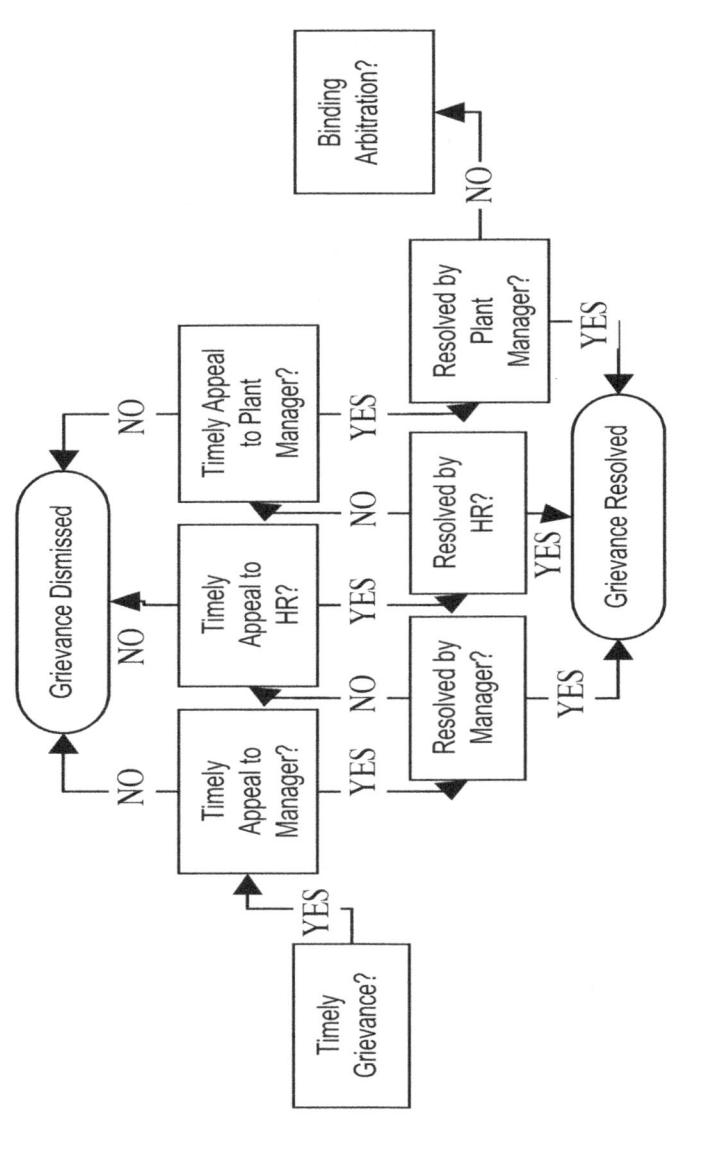

Sample Grievance Procedure

Section 1
A grievance within the meaning of the Article shall be limited to a dispute arising between the parties hereto involving interpretation of application of the provisions of this Agreement. Should a grievance arise it shall be handled in the following manner:

Step 1. The aggrieved employee, will present his grievance to his immediate supervisor within two (2) working days of the occurrence of the complained-of event. If not presented within this period, the case cannot be presented at a future date. The Company shall render a decision within seven (7) working days of the date of presentation.

Step 2. If not disposed of in Step 1, the employee may present the grievance in writing to the Company. A decision at Step 1 is final, and the grievance shall be withdrawn unless the grievance is taken to Step 2 within three (3) working days of the date of decision at Step 1. The Company shall give this decision within seven (7) working days after the grievance is presented to him.

Step 3. If not disposed of in Step 2, the employee and the business representative of the Union may appeal the grievance by giving written notice thereof to the Company. A decision at Step 2 shall be considered as final unless the notice of appeal to Step 3 is given within five (5) calendar days after the decision. The Company shall render this decision within seven (7) calendar days from the date the written grievance is presented at Step 3.

At any step of the grievance procedure, if the appropriate Company representative does not act within the specified period, the grievance shall be considered as having been denied as of conclusion of the applicable period.

Section 2
Only those issues fulfilling both of the following requirements can be appealed beyond Step 3.
    a. The grievance must be based on an alleged violation by the Company of a specific contract provision or must be based on the interpretation or application of a specific provision of the contract. A Company decision will not be subject to reversal unless it is found that the Company misinterpreted or violated the express terms of the contract.
b. The grievance must have been processed through each step of the grievance procedure in a timely manner unless it has been mutually agreed in writing by both parties that a specific step is to be bypassed or time limits waived.

Section 3
If the decision of the Company in Step 3 is unsatisfactory to the Union, and the Union wishes to process the grievance further, the Union must make a written request to the Company within seven (7) calendar days following the Step 3

decision. The written request shall include a specific statement of the violations and the position of the Union concerning the Union's interpretation of the disputed contract provision along with the specific remedy requested.

Section 4
Appeal of a Step 3 decision shall be to the President of the Company who shall have the final authority to render a decision on the matter. If the matter remains unresolved at this point the parties may, subject to the jurisdictional standards of Section 7, appeal the matter to binding arbitration.

Section 5
All grievance matters shall be handled at a time other than normal working hours, and shall not interfere with an employee's performance of his duties. Time spent by the employee in handling such matters shall be without pay.

Section 6
No employee or Union representative shall in any manner solicit or encourage grievances and disputes.

Section 7
Disputes involving the interpretation or application of the provisions of this Agreement are subject to arbitration. Matters involving employee grievances shall be brought to formal arbitration only after attempts to resolve the grievance in the steps as outlined in the Grievance Procedure are completed.

Section 8
When the Union invokes the arbitration procedure, the Union will request a panel of arbitrators from the Federal Mediation and Conciliation Service. The FMCS shall send the list of arbitrators to the authorized representatives of the Union and the Company. The arbitrator will be selected from the panel by the parties, alternately striking a name until a single arbitrator is selected. The party to strike the first name shall be determined by the toss of a coin. Either party reserves the right to reject only one list from the FMCS and request another list prior to striking of names. The Arbitrator shall conduct a hearing as expeditiously as is possible and shall render his decision promptly and without undue delay. The decision of the Arbitrator shall be final and binding on both parties.

Section 9
During hearings before the arbitrator, the Company and the Union shall be afforded a full opportunity to present any evidence, written or oral, which may be pertinent to the matter before the arbitrator. Each party shall bear their own expenses. The fees of the arbitrator shall be borne by the losing party. The arbitrator shall only interpret the Agreement and shall not modify, amend, add to or delete from any of its provisions in deciding the issue(s) submitted to him by the parties as contained in the above grievance procedure.

Section 10
Employees covered by this Agreement cannot, except through the duly constituted officials of the Union, initiate the arbitration procedures set forth in this Article. No arbitration award shall grant relief extending beyond the termination date of this contract, nor be retroactive beyond the date upon which the difference was first presented to the Company.

Responding to Grievances

What do you do if a grievance is filed against you? When a grievance is brought to the company, it is normally done in writing. Most grievance procedures require that the company's response also be in writing.

There is some art involved in responding to grievances. Managers who respond to grievances need to know the best defenses to common grievances. The one the company chooses can have a significant impact on whether the parties resolve the grievance at a low level or whether it goes to arbitration. The defense used by the company will also either restrict or provide leeway for an arbitrator to decide. In most cases, the company would prefer the arbitrator have a narrow area of review when reaching a decision. This makes the possible range of decisions more predictable.

Best Defenses for Grievances

Let's look at the five best defenses for grievances in the preferred order you will want to use them.

1. **The Grievance is Untimely:** Probably the best defense to a grievance is that it is untimely. Most grievance procedures have a provision that states when a grievance must be submitted to be considered. For example, it's common for a grievance procedure to say that a grievance submitted to the company more than five days after the occurrence is untimely. The employee automatically waives a claim filed six days after the incident. This is one of the best management defenses because it is relatively cut and dried. If the incident that prompted the grievance happened outside the five-day window, an arbitrator has no jurisdiction to review the claim. Therefore, it must be rejected.

2. **Grievance Does Not Allege Violation of Contract:** If the union files the grievance within the required timeframe, then the next best defense is that the complaint does not allege a violation of the contract. Arbitrators are only allowed to review grievances that develop directly from the terms of the collective bargaining agreement. An arbitrator is not authorized to consider a situation outside some provision of the contract. This defense is superior to most other defenses because, like the time-limit defense, it is a jurisdictional question. If an arbitrator concludes that the contract does not speak to the grievance, then he

or she does not have to look at any of the facts surrounding the actual grievance. This defense, however, is inferior to the time-limit defense because what the contract provisions are often less certain than the timeliness of a complaint.

3. **No Violation—Contract Allows Management Action**: The next best defense to a grievance is just to claim that management did not violate the contract. If the company can point to a contract provision that required the action taken, this should be a successful defense. This is somewhat inferior to the jurisdictional defenses because it raises factual issues. These cases can be extremely complicated when a labor agreement has conflicting provisions. The union relies on the wording of one clause for its actions, and the company relies on the language of a separate clause to justify what it did. Two equally plausible interpretations of the same language in the contract can also cause complications. These factors create a certain amount of subjectivity and room for maneuvering on the part of the arbitrator.

4. **Act Within Management's Rights—Past Practice:** The next best defense is to claim the company's actions are consistent with past practice or are within management's rights. This defense rests on management's right to manage the workplace as provided for in the union contract, which trumps any violation alleged by the union. These cases usually end up in front of an arbitrator because they are so fact-dependent.

5. **Factually Untrue:** The hardest defense to win is to claim the complaint is not true. The disadvantage of this defense is that it assumes if what the union is saying is correct, then management agrees that it should lose the grievance. The crux of this defense is that while the union is alleging something that violates the contract, the facts do not support the union's claim. In other words, the union is lying. This is a difficult defense to prove. It relies on statements of witnesses and other documentary evidence. The arbitrator decides these cases after hearing witnesses for both sides. Each side offers different versions of the facts, which means arbitrators must decide these cases based on credibility.

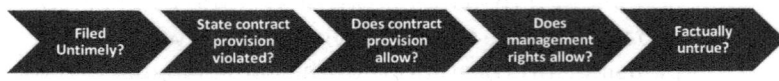

What to Do When a Grievance Is Filed

Now that you know the best defenses, what do you do if an employee files a grievance against you? Here are seven key steps:

1. **Investigate the Complaint:** Like any other complaint lodged by an employee in either union or non-union environments, the first step is to investigate the grievance thoroughly. Accumulate any available documentary evidence, interview possible witnesses,

and review the company's history of dealing with similar situations.

2. **Review the Contract for Favorable Language:** You must identify whether there is any contract language that supports the employee's claim. You will need to review not only the contract provisions the employee relies on, if any, but also review the contract for areas that justify whatever action was taken by the company.

3. **Review Grievant's Personnel File:** Next, you will want to look at the grievant's personnel file. This is especially important in cases where the issue concerns disciplinary action taken against the employee. You will need a good picture of the individual's prior work history—did the employee have any knowledge of the work rule or contract provision in question?

4. **Document Everything:** After interviewing all witnesses, be sure you document the information you've gathered.

5. **Don't Commit To "Past Practice" Without Approval:** Also, when responding to a grievance, do not commit to "past practice" without top management approval. This is discussed in detail later in this book.

6. **Keep Your Response Brief:** Your response to a grievance should be short. A wordy response creates more areas for the union or an arbitrator to pick apart the decision. Just state that the company

denies the grievance. If there's a contractual basis for the denial, identify the contract provision on which management is relying. A typical grievance response might say, "Grievance denied; management's action allowed under Article 2 Management's Rights."

7. **Watch the Time Limits:** When responding to grievances, look at all time limits. Under some grievance procedures if management fails to respond in time it loses the chance to appeal. The company gets stuck with the outcome. Although most contracts state that a grievance management does not answer within the time limits is considered denied, it's nevertheless a good idea to make sure to respond to grievances in a timely fashion.

If you can't resolve the grievance, you may have to defend your decision in front of an arbitrator. The most severe cases are terminations, and they have an extraordinary level of review called "just cause." We will learn about that in the next chapter.

CHAPTER 3
Just Cause

What is Just Cause?

"Just cause" is probably the most important legal concept you need to learn as a manager in a union shop. In virtually all union contracts an employee cannot be fired except for "just cause."

Comparison to "At-Will" Employment

To help better understand the concept let's compare "just cause" to "at-will" employment. Virtually every court in the country presumes that either party may terminate an employment relationship at their will. In other words, an employee can leave their job at any time for any reason, and that an employer may terminate that employee at any time for any reason. There are exceptions to this rule, most significantly that termination cannot occur for an illegal reason (i.e. a company cannot fire an at-will employee because of his race or her gender).

But in labor contracts the rules are different. Virtually all labor agreements state that the employment relationship may not be terminated "at will," but instead may only be terminated for what is called "just cause." Just cause is a legal concept developed over the years in thousands of arbitration decisions that helps to define when companies can terminate the employment relationship in unionized settings. For management to get an arbitrator to uphold a decision to fire a union-represented worker, it must satisfy the burden of proving that the decision was for "just cause."

The Three Tests for "Just Cause"

There are three main factors an arbitrator will consider when deciding whether a termination was for just cause.

1. **"Did the employee breach or commit the offense?"** This is the basic factual question the arbitrator must resolve in any determination of just cause—did the act occur?

2. **"Did the offense warrant punishment?"** Next, the arbitrator must determine whether the act or offense warranted the corrective action or punishment. In answering this question, the arbitrator is not looking so much at the level of discipline (i.e. was the employee terminated, suspended or given a verbal warning) but is more interested in whether the act is something that deserves to be corrected. When deciding this question, the arbitrator will consider whether the employee was aware that what they did could result in corrective action, was there a rule against what they did, and did they violate the contract.

3. **"Was the penalty appropriate?"** Finally, the arbitrator asks whether the penalty imposed is suitable for the employee's action or offense. In

other words, does the punishment fit the crime? Even if some corrective action was justified, the arbitrator might nevertheless decide that what management did, in this case, was excessive or unfair.

Factors Used to Determine Just Cause

Arbitrators look at numerous factors when deciding whether the employer met the "just cause" burdens.

1. **Was employee warned?** The arbitrator will consider whether the employee knew the consequences of their conduct. Management may want to show evidence that the employee received prior written warnings regarding the same conduct. You could show proof of bulletin board postings or training sessions where the employee learned the rule. Work rules, and documentation that other employees received similar punishment and that this was known, all help to prove that the employee was aware of the potential consequences of their actions.

2. **Is work rule related to important business reason?** An arbitrator will consider whether the company rule is reasonably related to the efficient and safe operation of the firm. Even if employees knew about the rule, an arbitrator would still be reluctant to apply punishment if the requirement is not consequential to the efficient operation of the business. This is obviously a judgment call. Some arbitrators feel management should be able to adopt any rules it believes are related to the efficient operation of the

company, while other arbitrators take a strict view of the things companies can and should require of employees. In either case, it's important that you justify the business reasons for certain disciplinary actions.

3. **Did management conduct a full and fair investigation?** An arbitrator also decides whether management conducted a full, fair, and objective investigation. The best proof of this are the notes and other documentation collected by the manager who conducted the investigation. If a memo was drafted that summarizes the results, that is also good proof. But there must be further evidence that the investigation was thorough, fair, and objective. Just because one occurred does not necessarily mean the company is home free. Management needs to prove that it did not simply take one side of the story as being gospel. You must show that full credence was given to the defense of the grieved employee. You should demonstrate that the company interviewed witnesses sympathetic to the worker's side of the story.

If credibility is the reason management believes one side of the story over another, it is important that you explain why some witnesses are more credible than others. This explanation should go beyond just stating that one person is more truthful than another person. Raise issues of motives, body language, and inconsistencies. Conclusions based on a thorough investigation of this sort will be tough for an arbitrator to ignore. By the same token, a decision that is made without an investigation, even if that decision was entirely correct, can be overturned by an arbitrator because management did not conduct a full, fair, and objective investigation.

4. **Substantial evidence of guilt?** The arbitrator will consider whether there is evidence of guilt. The burden of proof in workplace termination situations is one of "substantial evidence." There must be a significant amount of evidence pointing to the conclusion that the violation occurred, as opposed to only a small amount of proof. Again, this should come out during a thorough investigation. You will hopefully have documentary evidence, eye-witness accounts, and other evidence that proves the employee committed a violation.

    The burden of proof for "substantial evidence" is lower than the "beyond a reasonable doubt" standard found in criminal courts. Occasionally, an arbitrator will apply the stricter "beyond a reasonable doubt" standard. If an employee allegedly committed a violation that is criminal in nature, such as a drug-related offense or theft, an arbitrator may apply the higher burden of proof due to the fact the employee may be subject to additional criminal charges after the arbitration hearing. But in most cases, management is permitted to act, even if there is a small amount of doubt as to whether the employee committed a violation, if there is "substantial evidence."

5. **Was punishment applied consistently?** Arbitrators always look at whether the penalty was applied consistently. If management has responded to the same or similar circumstances with different discipline in the past, an arbitrator is unlikely to approve of more strict or severe punishment. Under certain circumstances, an arbitrator may allow management to change the way it has applied penalties. This is more likely when there is a history of increasing problems over the same issue that has led management to clearly communicate that it is going to change the way discipline is applied. However, typically an arbitrator will either deny management's right to use a different punishment for a similar circumstance or reduce the penalty to be consistent with prior punishments applied in similar situations.

While employers have the discretion to set rules of conduct within the parameters of collective bargaining agreements, rules must be published and well communicated. It is not enough to say that a rule existed if an employee can argue that they had no knowledge of it or that management never enforced the rule. Many arbitrators will disallow disciplinary action on that basis. Also, there should be consistent enforcement. When a rule has not been applied, or has been enforced to varying degrees, an arbitrator is unlikely to uphold disciplinary action.

6. **Does the punishment fit the crime?** The last thing the arbitrator will look at is whether the penalty is reasonably related to the seriousness of the offense and the employee's record. In other words, does the punishment fit the crime? The arbitrator will look at the employee's record or performance, including any prior disciplinary actions. An employee with a "clean record" will be given more leeway than one who has a history of not following company directions. The arbitrator will also consider similar cases at other companies to determine whether the punishment that management is asking for is common in other organizations.

   An arbitrator looks at the disciplinary action as being corrective, not punitive. The idea behind a disciplinary action is to encourage good performance by employees in the unit and not only to punish them when they have done something wrong. If discipline does not appear to attempt to correct behavior or encourage good performance, but instead appears punitive, an arbitrator may refuse to enforce that punishment. For this reason, it is important that managers avoid arbitrary or hasty actions.

Creating a Good Record

Arbitrators want to see evidence of a thoughtful and considerate approach to any disciplinary decision. This might include more than one attempt by management to communicate with the employee about deficiencies in their performance before disciplinary action occurring. Decisions made in haste are often not the best decisions. Management should be able to prove that it took a considered approach in designing disciplinary action. Part of this process includes evaluating the discipline considering the employee's record and seniority.

The Role of Seniority

A long-term employee with no record of problems is not likely to have disciplinary action upheld against him or her for a first-time infraction of a rule. In most cases, and particularly with long-term employees, there will need to be a record of problem performance before an arbitrator finds just cause. At the same time, an arbitrator won't hold an employee with little or no experience to the same standard as longer-term employees regarding knowledge of rules and procedures. For these reasons, each incident needs to be carefully examined, and disciplinary action should be related to the employee's prior work performance and experience.

Combining Offenses

Managers sometimes want to discipline an employee for conduct that is related to, but not precisely the same as, something the employee did in the past. For example, a manager may want to combine attendance infractions with other infractions. Arbitrators, however, are very careful about combining offenses. Typically, they use a concept called "comparable offense" when deciding these cases. For an offense to be considered equivalent, and therefore capable of being combined with other disciplinary action, the arbitrator will want to see that the breach is related to a similar work rule or contract provision and not a wholly separate area.

In the example just cited, if the first disciplinary warning was for attendance and the second disciplinary warning was for quality control issues, it is unlikely the arbitrator will uphold combining the two disciplinary actions. On the other hand, if one warning was for tardiness while a second warning was for absenteeism, many arbitrators will find these offenses to be comparable and therefore capable of being combined.

If offenses are non-comparable, then the arbitrator will insist that the company handle each disciplinary action independently. For this reason, managers should be careful when combining offenses and should only connect incidents that are reasonably similar. An exception to this rule is in workplaces where the contract provides for disciplinary action on multiple active disciplinary warnings. For example, some contracts state that employees are not allowed to bid on new jobs if they have four or more current disciplinary actions in their file at one time, and those four incidents may be unrelated.

The "12-month" Rule of Thumb

Finally, avoid combining offenses when one or more of the offenses are over 12 months old. In certain circumstances, especially when a contract specifies an offense will be on an employee's record for longer than a year, you can extend the warnings. However, most arbitrators will not allow employers to combine disciplinary actions when one of the offenses occurred more than 12 months before the current event.

Accelerating Offenses

Managers often like to accelerate steps in the disciplinary action process, and sometimes want to go straight to suspension or even termination. Arbitrators will look closely at situations where a manager wants to skip steps in the disciplinary action process, especially when the manager wants the employee terminated without prior disciplinary action.

The arbitrator will look at the gravity of the offense. Things like workplace violence, drug or alcohol abuse, and theft may be considered appropriate areas for the immediate termination without prior warning. Outside of this handful of extreme situations, an arbitrator is unlikely to accept immediate termination, although they might approve an initial suspension or other accelerated disciplinary action.

Besides the gravity of the offense, the arbitrator will look at all the circumstances surrounding the offense. These might include whether other issues in the work environment aggravated the employee or whether some extenuating facts or circumstances mitigate the action in question. Another factor to be considered is the employee's seniority and past work record. Like in normal just cause situations, an arbitrator will review any prior misconduct by an employee when deciding whether disciplinary action is appropriate. If the company accelerates punishment against an employee with a good record, she is more likely to be reinstated by an arbitrator. A related consideration is a past practice or precedent. If other similar misconduct in the past did not lead to termination, it is unlikely an arbitrator will uphold a dismissal now.

The arbitrator will lastly consider how accelerating discipline serves to correct the employee. Again, the arbitrator will ask whether termination best serves to remedy the employee and prevent future misconduct. For example, management can make a compelling argument that a verbal or written warning for a serious safety violation does not send the correct message and may even signal employees that management does not take safety seriously. Thus, management can show that accelerating discipline sends a more appropriate message.

How to Write a Defensible Written Reprimand

Here is a quick guide to writing a written reprimand that will be defensible under your grievance procedure.

1. **Include All Material Facts:** First, list all the facts, including especially the date, the time, the act or omission that is the basis for the discipline, and all documentation related to the incident.

2. **Quote the Rule and Contract Provision Violated:** Quote the rule or contract provision you believe the employee or union violated.

3. **List Any Prior Discipline:** Include any previous warnings, counseling, or other caution given in the last 12 months that are comparable to the current

issue.

4. **"This Constitutes a Written Reprimand":** State explicitly that this constitutes a written reprimand.

5. **Opportunity to Correct:** State that the reprimand gives the employee an opportunity to correct his or her behavior.

6. **Further Disciplinary Action:** State that the employee will be subject to further disciplinary action, up to and including termination, if he or she fails to correct their conduct in the future.

Sample Written Reprimand

January 23, 2003

Dear John Doe:

This letter constitutes a written reprimand regarding your abuse of the excused absence procedure under our labor agreement with Widget Workers Local 007.

As we discussed today, you are already on a final warning for unexcused absences. Over the past several weeks you have provided many faxed doctor's notes from a Dr. Jack Kevorkian, D.O. in Southfield, Michigan to excuse several recent absences. It is unclear why a doctor in Michigan is treating you here in Missouri. Based on my investigation this doctor has faxed several excuses without physically seeing you for treatment. This is exceedingly unusual and appears to be an attempt to "game" our labor agreement.

Our labor agreement states in Article XII(d) as follows: "Absences will only be excused if accompanied by a note from a treating physician stating the reason for the absence and the expected date of return." A note from a doctor in Michigan, who has not physically seen you for treatment, does not meet the language of Article XII(d).

Your attendance at work is very important. It is critical for us to be able to count on you to meet the needs of our customers. We understand that you want to keep your job and we hope you can keep it. However, it is not fair to your co-workers, who must follow the attendance policy and must cover for you when you are not here, to continue to let you receive excuses from a doctor who cannot even physically see you for treatment.

Based on your excessive absenteeism, the number of doctor's excuses in addition to your unexcused absences, and your apparent attempt to circumvent our labor contract, I want to clarify what counts as a valid excused absence. For a doctor's note to be accepted you must provide a note from a treating physician who examines you in person. We will not excuse absences based on a note from a doctor who treats you over the phone. Failure to adhere to these requirements will result in additional disciplinary action, up to and including termination.

Employee		Date	
Company		Date	
Union Steward		Date	

Communication—Witnesses

Be sure to notify the employee and the union of a reprimand. During any investigation that might lead to disciplinary action, it is important to remember that the union member has a right to be represented by a steward or another union representative. This is known as the employee's *Weingarten* rights, and management is required to allow a witness if requested. If the employee does not request a witness in the disciplinary meeting, management does not have to provide one.

Mail a copy of the reprimand to the employee, or give it to them personally. If mailed, send it certified with return receipt requested. If you had it to the employee, ask the employee to sign a receipt stating that they received the reprimand. If the employee refuses to sign a receipt, have a witness document that the employee was given a receipt but refused to sign it.

Mail a copy of the reprimand to the union's place of business; your human resources department may handle this. Also, deliver a copy to the union shop steward and document that the steward received the reprimand. Finally, note the reprimand in the employee's work record by including a copy in their personnel file.

Follow these suggestions and your disciplinary and termination decisions are likely to be upheld by an arbitrator if ever challenged by the union.

CHAPTER 4
Past Practice and Erosion

Past practice and the related concept of contract erosion are two of the most important in managing a unionized environment. In a nutshell, past practice refers to the history of actions taken either by management or the union, actions that are relied upon by the parties to resolve similar issues in the future. Erosion refers to the idea that management (and sometimes unions) can lose the right to act in a certain way due to their past practice. In other words, the company's actions can be limited by what it has done or allowed in the past, no matter what the language in a collective bargaining agreement says.

Management Rights in the "State of Nature"

Erosion refers to any action or inaction by management which serves to reduce its authority to manage under the union contract. Perhaps the best way to think of erosion is to think about management's rights <u>before</u> the contract existed. Before a union contract, management has the unfettered right to manage its business. I call this the "state of nature."

In the state of nature, management has the right to manage that organization however it sees fit, so long as it is not breaking the law. Management can change wages, hours or working conditions in any way that it believes will help it to achieve its business objectives.

When a union comes in the state of nature changes. Management can no longer make unilateral changes to wages, hours or conditions of employment. It first must bargain regarding those changes with the labor organization. While this does not prohibit the company from acting, it is one additional step management must take before acting. Further, once the company enters a labor agreement, its right to act can become further limited. The terms of the collective bargaining agreement can restrict management's ability to act per the provisions of that contract. Therefore, management's right has been limited even further from the original state of nature.

An Example of Erosion

Let me give you an example of contract erosion. If the labor agreement states, for example, that management will give 24-hour notice to the union before requiring overtime, management is not allowed to require overtime with less than 24-hour notice. If, during the administration of the contract, the managers routinely give 48-hour notice before requiring overtime, this can create a problem. If it becomes a consistent past practice (we will talk about this in more detail below) the union can argue that management has further limited its right to act even though the contract states that the company is only required to give 24-hour notice. If managers create a solid past practice, then managers have eroded the rights of the company through the labor agreement.

The key point to remember is that management is only required to do what the contract states. In most collective bargaining agreements management maintains its rights that existed in the "state of nature" before the contract existed.

No "Gifts"

There are occasions where routine management decisions can become "gifts" to the union, like the example earlier about giving extra notice for overtime. Over time these "gifts" can become binding on management. Another way erosion occurs is through caving into union demands. If the union continuously files grievances over an issue and management finally stops pressing for its interpretation, management has caved into the union's demand and will be stuck with the union's interpretation of that contract provision.

Grievance Settlements and Erosion

Management can erode its rights further by grievance settlements and arbitration decisions. If management settles several grievances the same way, it can be bound to those contract interpretations in the future. This is true, even where management states explicitly that its grievance settlement will not have any precedent value in the future.

Many managers find this result unfair. An arbitrator who is brought in from outside to review the working relationship between the parties is not necessarily bound by what parties say in grievance settlements, even if the parties agree the settlement will have no precedent value in the future. While some arbitrators may decide to enforce that language, others will look to the history of the relationship between the parties. If every time management has faced a problem they resolved it the same way, an arbitrator may find that in the interest of peace and predictability between the parties it makes more sense to require management to address the issue the same way every time.

Why <u>You</u> Are Most Likely to Erode Your Contract

It is important for managers to be aware that they are the most likely individuals in the company to erode management's rights. This is because managers are the ones that enforce and sometimes fail to enforce contract provisions every day. It is very important for the manager to remember to follow the contract provisions carefully and make sure that they do everything that is required by the contract and yet nothing more than what is required by the contract.

Past Practice

Past practice is like a "precedent" in our court system. While an arbitrator is not always bound by the past practice of the parties when reaching a decision, past practice is certainly a valuable tool used by arbitrators to determine the proper outcome of grievances.

What is past practice? Past practice is created by supervisors, managers or by the leadership of the union. For our purposes, we will talk about past practice solely from the standpoint of managers. It is important to understand that the union officials can also create past practice. Managers also exercise their "right to manage" and create past practice by administering and applying the written contract.

Most labor contracts include broad management rights authority. When managers act based on this "management right to act" they are creating past practice. Past practice is used to flesh out the skeleton of the written contract. It supplements the written clauses, standards, and procedures outlined in the collective bargaining agreement. Management relies on past practice any time the written agreement does not expressly decide an issue. The union, on the other hand, will rely on past practice to try to maintain work conditions as they existed before the contract or to seek to hold management to past exceptions.

Where Does Past Practice Come From?

There are many sources of past practice in an organization. Managers create past practice during isolated situations where a manager is forced to act in circumstances unforeseen by the individuals who bargained the collective bargaining agreement. For example, a large one-time order from a customer may require you to add emergency staff for a short period, something not covered in your collective bargaining agreement. What do you do? The procedure you develop in this situation may create a past practice that will bind the company in the future.

Even where the contract anticipates situations, special circumstances may require a manager to make a decision that adds to or subtracts from language in the contract. Building on the earlier example, pretend that your contract did foresee emergency staffing situations, but only authorizes emergency staffing for one week. At the time the contract was negotiated there had never been an instance where the company used emergency staff for more than one week, so the provision worked well. However, a customer approaches your business to take on a special project that will last only a month, but will require emergency staffing. How should the company respond?

If you follow the emergency procedure in the contract your company is creating facts that may require it to use that process any time it needs emergency staffing. On the other hand, if the company adopts a new procedure the union may complain about the change. Each situation is unique and factors such as internal union politics and prior grievances or complaints may affect how the parties respond.

Uncommon Occurrences and Equivocal Actions

A common saying of lawyers is that bad facts make bad law, and the same thing can be true about the "law of the shop." Uncommon or isolated occurrences that the collective bargaining agreement doesn't cover require managers to act on their feet. Often the easiest or most direct solution in these instances is not the best option in the long term. If a manager or supervisor fails to think through the potential consequences of the decision, it can have long-term ramifications on the organization.

Managers can also generate past practice by taking "equivocal" actions. In other words, a manager who wants to repay an employee for doing them a favor at some other time may make exceptions to the rule. Those exceptions can, over time, become accepted past practice and end up modifying terms of the collective bargaining agreement.

The Problem with Past Practice

Think about it like this. When companies and unions sit down to negotiate a collective bargaining agreement, the process can take months and sometimes even a year or more. The reason it takes so long is not just the process of give and take. They analyze each proposal carefully. They consider the future impact on the business. Each must be considered from the standpoint of its potential costs, its impact on production and anticipating how the other party will respond to it. A very important skill in collective bargaining is predicting how the other party will respond to contract proposals and including in counter-proposals language to try to account for those reactions.

The problem with making decisions on-the-fly is that those decisions often do not have a chance to go through the rigorous analysis that contract proposals go through. Unfortunately, on the fly decisions can have just as binding an impact on the organization as written provisions of the collective bargaining agreement itself. That's why past practice is so important for managers to understand.

How Past Practice Comes Up in Grievances

So how does past practice come up during the typical grievance process? For example, pretend an employee is denied a vacation request by his supervisor for time off during hunting season. His supervisor relies on contract language that states a manager may deny leave requests for various reasons, including hunting season. However, over the years managers of the company have routinely approved vacation requests for hunting season.

When the supervisor denies the leave request, the employee files a grievance noting that managers routinely approved vacation requests for hunting season in the past. If you were an arbitrator, how would you review that situation? Most will start with the language of the collective bargaining agreement. An arbitrator's job is to interpret and enforce the language of the collective bargaining agreement. However, an arbitrator will also look to the "fixed and established" past practice of the employer when determining the outcome of a case.

"Fixed and Established" Past Practice

There are four standards an arbitrator will use when determining whether there is a "fixed and established" past practice. The four standards considered are whether the action of management is unequivocal, clearly enunciated, existed over a reasonably extended period and accepted and acted upon by both parties' line representatives. Let's look at each in turn.

1. **Is the practice unequivocal?** The past practice must be granted or applied consistently, uniformly, regularly and without a break. In our example, the arbitrator would want to know how many times the employer has approved vacation requests for hunting season and whether the company had ever denied a leave request for hunting season. If the company has denied them in the past, the arbitrator will want to know the circumstances. The fewer examples the company can show where it refused such requests, the more likely the arbitrator will rule that the practice of granting vacation requests for hunting season is unequivocal.

2. **Is it clearly communicated?** The arbitrator in our example will want to know whether the company clearly communicated the practice of granting leave requests for hunting season. For example, were memos posted where the employer put conditions on approval of vacation requests for hunting season? Have these conditions ever been announced in employee meetings? These are important facts to know. Any other clear communication that shows the company reserved the right to deny vacation requests during hunting season is favorable.

3. **Did the practice exist over an extended period?** Next, the arbitrator will determine whether the practice existed over a reasonably long period. He or she will decide this case-by-case. In some cases, a month or two might be enough experience; in others, it may be years. Since most hunting seasons only occur on a yearly basis, an arbitrator may need to see

several years of activity before making a conclusion about this issue. In our example, there are several years during which the employer approved vacation requests for hunting season. This appears to meet the "length of time" requirement.

4. **Is the practice accepted and acted upon?** Finally, the arbitrator will want to know whether the past practice has been accepted and acted upon by both parties through their line representatives. Facts that show that one party acquiesced to the actions of the other is important. The history of approving vacation requests for hunting seasons shows some level of acquiescence by the employer in our example. However, if there are cases where the employer denied leave requests for hunting season the arbitrator will be especially interested in how the parties reacted to that. If there is proof that the company rejected vacation requests in the past over hunting season and that the Union did not grieve, that may be evidence of acquiescence on the part of the union.

Using the Grievance Record to Evaluate Past Practice

Arbitrators will often use old grievances between the parties to determine past practice. They will look primarily at three areas:

1. **The written grievance record:** What did the grievance claim? The original written grievance may

be used to prove past practice. It certainly demonstrates the state of mind of the grieving party regarding the contract provision. It is especially useful for showing whether the parties acquiesced to a particular interpretation of the contract. If a grievance alleges the company has a regular practice, the company's response should deny this statement if untrue. A commitment in a grievance response on past practice, even if it is inaccurate, can be used against the company in future grievances or arbitration hearings as proof of what the company practice was.

2. **The answer to grievances:** Next, the arbitrator may look at the written grievance answers. The answers to grievances often can be used to prove what the parties believed were the terms of the contract. Even if the company can show other occasions where it did not follow that practice, the grievance response certainly would be evidence of at least one manager's view on the issue. This proof could be used by the union to show the arbitrator that the parties did accept that past practice.

3. **The grievance settlement record:** Have there been other prior grievances on this same issue and how were those settled? A history of grievances between the parties over an issue shows that there is not acquiescence or an unequivocal past practice.

How A Company Can Overcome Past Practice

So, what happens if the company creates past practice and wants to change it? Again, using our example of vacation requests, let's pretend that the firm believes it created a past practice and the contract provision regarding hunting season is no longer enforceable because of the actions of some managers. How can it overcome the past practice?

1. **Change it at the Bargaining Table:** One way the employer could change this past practice is to change it at the bargaining table. The company could propose during the next bargaining negotiations that it will deny requests for vacation during hunting season. This gives the employer a clean slate and clearly states that the old past practice is no longer the rule.

    The advantage of using the bargaining table to deal with past practice is that it is absolutely clear. Both parties can negotiate and during the give and take of the negotiation process they come to an agreement on the new rule. The disadvantage of trying to change past practice at the bargaining table is that it can result in further cementing that past practice.

    If the company goes into negotiations and asks for the no time off for hunting provision, but the union refuses to agree to that clause, the company is stuck. In a future arbitration, there is no way the arbitrator will uphold the company's claim. The union will use the evidence of what occurred during collective bargaining as proof that the union did not acquiesce to the company's position and that the company believed at that time that the contract did not contain this provision. In this case the past practice of approving vacations for hunting season would prevail.

2. **Posting or communicating the rule:** If the past practice occurs because of failure to enforce a rule or a rule becomes dormant, the company can re-establish the rule by posting it and making it known to both the employees and the union as a new rule. This action responds directly to the standard of whether the action is clearly enunciated. If acted upon, posting the new notice also deals with the other four standards of being unequivocal, existing over an extended period and being accepted or acted upon by the parties. The disadvantage of this approach is that it gives the union an immediate opportunity to file a grievance and to attack the new rule. This makes the company vulnerable since the facts of the past practice will often prevail. Often the company's purpose is to go ahead and have the fight about the issue, so they post the rule in hopes they will prevail with an arbitrator.

3. **Denying grievances:** The company can also overcome past practice by just denying grievances or using counter-grievance settlements to create an equivocal situation regarding a contract provision. In our example, the company could begin to refuse vacation requests or to deny grievances on the issue of vacation for hunting season. This creates a

pattern of equivocal responses. This record will then be used to show an arbitrator there was not a fixed and established past practice. The company's hope is that the arbitrator will decide to rely on the express language of the written contract and not the union's claim of a fixed and established past practice.

4. **Change the operation:** Finally, the company could change its operation such that the procedures that gave rise to the past practice no longer exist. Again, using our example, the company might change the way that its shifts operate such that employees who want time off during hunting season can select a shift to receive time off without requiring vacation requests. This operational change then makes the grievance issue go away without dealing with whether the contract provision or past practice continues to exist.

Past practice in the unionized environment makes the job of the supervisor much more challenging. In your role as contract administrator it is not nearly enough to just follow the rules outlined in the collective bargaining agreement. Also, you are required to make sure that when exercising your management right that you do so with an eye toward protecting the company's flexibility and right to manage in the future.

Commitments made under the auspices of the management rights clause can become as binding as a contract provision. For that reason, it is important for managers to not only know the contract, but to have a strong bias toward protecting management's flexibility and its right to manage. If you can do this, you are well on your way to being an effective manager in a union environment.

CHAPTER 5
Leading in a Union Shop

A lot of managers in union shops don't think much about leadership. Some believe the labor contract removes a lot of their flexibility or motivational tools available to non-union managers. But that view is short-sighted.

If anything, the role of leadership in union shops is even *great*er than in non-union ones. Union officials will often try to create an "us versus them" attitude to divide front line employees from their managers. Cultures like that are less productive, more hostile, and often kill companies.

But we've learned that as a leader in a union shop you have a surprising amount of flexibility and tools to build a solid work culture. It is often up to you to create that culture. A place where teammates help each other out, perform "above and beyond" work, and build and grow a successful business.

Leadership is hard, especially in a union shop. Some days—like after helping an employee through a rough patch or watching your team rise to the occasion and reach a big goal—you feel like you've got it nailed. Other days (if you're anything like me) you wonder if you know anything about leadership at all. It can be a struggle.

As the head of my own business I coach, praise, encourage, discipline, listen to, celebrate, and yes, sometimes even fire, employees. On top of that, many of our consulting clients turn to us for help with their employee relations issues and leadership crises.

My views about what works (and doesn't work) I learned in the trenches—and it's during the toughest times that you see the best leaders shine. After watching some leaders succeed and others fall flat on their faces, I started asking a question you've probably asked too: *What separates good leaders from those who fail?*

It turns out this question isn't so easy to answer. Many people who seem like they'd be great leaders are horrible. And then there are others you underestimate as "not leadership material," only to discover that their people would run into a burning building for them. What often makes the difference is something I call Approachable Leadership.

Approachable Leadership represents a set of day-to-day habits great leaders use to build a connection with the people they lead. It's something different from charisma, personality, leadership style, or emotional intelligence. It's a way of engaging that forges deeper connections, builds trust, and makes commitment possible.

What's more, we've discovered that Approachable Leadership can be learned. It is the best framework I've found to explain what separates the leaders who crumble from the ones who come out of the crucible hard as steel.

It is beyond to scope of this book to lay out all the principles and practices of Approachable Leadership. If you are interested in learning more, I encourage you to get a copy of my book *The Approachability Playbook: 3 Essential Habits for Thriving Leaders and Teams* (check out the end of the book for more information). But I want to introduce you to the model and to one important tool that can help you immediately improve your leadership skills.

The Connection Model: The Three Pillars of Approachable Leadership

Are you likely to succeed as a leader? The best way to tell is to look at your relationships. Leadership starts with connection. Approachable leaders stand out through the connections they share with the people they lead. They engage in daily habits that build up (rather than erode) connection.

The Connection Model describes how leaders can use approachable behavior to build a connection with co-workers. Here's how we define Approachable Leadership:

Approachable leaders connect with others by being *Open, Understanding, and Supportive*

These behaviors form the three pillars of Approachable Leadership.

The Connection Model

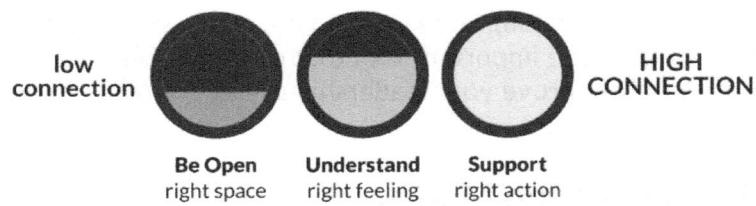

You can express each of these behaviors through habits you can learn and practice every day. Approachable Leaders show:

- **Openness** by being available, welcoming, and inviting—creating and maintaining "Right Space."
- **Understanding** through warmth, active listening, and empathy—exhibiting "Right Feeling."
- **Support** by being receptive to others, then following up and following through—performing "Right Action."

So how do you become more approachable? First, use a simple tool to assess the gaps in any relationship you have or are concerned about, and then begin to apply concrete action steps to increase your approachability (or to bridge the gap with someone you find unapproachable).

TOOL: Recognizing Approachability Gaps

Gaps between leaders and their teammates can cause major problems. But your employees won't just come up to you and tell you they are uncomfortable approaching you. Then how do you tell if there is a gap? This tool helps you recognize behavior that suggests a gap between you and a teammate.

There are three places where the gap might show up: (1) physical gaps, (2) verbal gaps, and (3) behavioral gaps (between what someone says and what they do). Use the assessment below to recognize signals of a gap. When you notice one, use the discussion starters to help shrink the gap.

Physical Gaps
If someone is uncomfortable with someone in power, it will often show up in their physical behavior. They will try to avoid the more powerful person.
- Physical distance, turned toward an "exit"
- Avoiding eye contact, looking at ceiling or floor
- Closed body language (arms crossed)
- Distracted, seems lost in thought
- Holding back or agitated body language

Verbal Gaps
These are the most common signals you will notice. Indirect or mitigated speech often expresses a power gap with a leader.

Watch for mitigated speech like:
- Hints ("I wonder if...")
- Preference ("perhaps we should...")
- Question ("do you think ___ would work?"), or

- Team suggestion ("why don't we try ___?")
- Look for attempts to "sugarcoat" or downplay bad news
- Being overly polite or deferential
- Quickly deferring or backing down when rejected by someone in power

Behavioral Gaps
Many times, actions speak louder than words. Watch for gaps between what someone says and what they do.

- Promising one thing, doing another
- No follow-through or follow-up
- Passive-aggressive actions
- Being "too busy" or procrastinating
- "Changing mind" about importance of issue

Discussion Starters
When you notice specific gaps, use the following discussion starters to help shrink the gap.

- "You seem uncomfortable. It's OK—I really want to know what you think."
- "I'm not 100% sure what I think about this myself. Tell me what you really think."
- "OK, that's what I do [name behavior] when I'm not sure if I should say something. What's up?"
- "I need your help. Can you be honest and tell me exactly what you think about this?"
- "I may be completely off base here, I don't know. Can you tell me what you really think?"

NOTE: This is just one of 6 tools in *The Approachability Playbook*. You can learn more and download all the tools mentioned in the book at **http://ALplaybook.com**

The Case for Approachability

We've watched leaders battle through their toughest situations. Some succeeded. Many failed. Over the years we've watched these leaders carefully and identified several simple habits that separate successful ones from the rest.

Over and over, we discovered that the thing that separated the successful leaders from those who did not fare as well was their approachability. New research shows that approachability delivers real business results in areas like:
- Cooperation
- Enthusiasm
- Employee commitment
- Workplace stress

A 2015 study from the University of Tulsa found that employees who rate their supervisor "approachable" are *89% more likely to report satisfaction with their work*. They also note better relationships with coworkers.

Employees of Approachable Leaders are happy and less stressed at work

Source: University of Tulsa, 2015

Plus, employees of approachable leaders are *more willing to go "above and beyond" at work*. They are 88% more likely to make suggestions or volunteer to pitch in outside their normal job. Behaviors like these improve cooperation, drive innovation and deliver business results.

Approachability predicts "above and beyond" behavior more than all other factors

Source: Journal of Management Development, 2005

Another surprising finding was that *approachability trumps other leader competencies*. Nearly 10% of the employees in this study had a low opinion of their supervisor. They went "above and beyond" anyway. The difference between these folks and those who let their frustration keep them on the sideline?

People who like their manager and are enthusiastic about their work don't quit.

These employees still felt their leader was approachable. It's that simple. That's why it's not surprising that the more approachable you are, the less likely your employees will consider leaving.

Employees of Approachable Leaders do not intend to quit their jobs

Source: University of Tulsa, 2015

Turnover wastes precious time, money, and energy. It frustrates everyone who must pick up the slack (especially your high performers, who you can least afford to lose). Approachable leaders put a stop to that negative cycle.

*This is just one of the studies cited in The Playbook. For more, see **http://approachableleadership.com/research**.*

Approachability is Teachable

There are thousands of things you can teach leaders. Trustworthiness and charisma (to name just two) are well-researched leader behaviors associated with positive business results.

No question these behaviors are desirable. But they are hard to affect through training. How do you reliably train someone to be more trustworthy? Or more charismatic?

Training "soft skill" basics (dealing with team dysfunction, conversation skills) is very useful, but often fails to get at the fundamental behaviors that reinforce strong leader relationships.

Approachable Leadership can solve this problem. It is simpler to learn, accessible, quickly understood, and easy to observe and practice. This makes it the **ideal habit for leaders to develop.**

Conclusion

Those are the basics you need to know to be an effective manager in a union shop. Good managers usually can't avoid grievances—let's face it, many grievances come up when a manager requires an employee to do something he or she doesn't want to do. And managers who never have a grievance filed against them may be "giving in" to union demands. However, if you keep these fundamental principles in mind, you will be able to do a good job as a manager and avoid making decisions that might hurt the company. You'll avoid most grievances. You'll win the ones that do get filed. Good luck!

Notes

Notes

Notes

Notes

Bring Managing the Union Shop to <u>Your</u> Company!

Smart unions know that *real negotiations* begin the day <u>after</u> a contract is signed – this is where unions take advantage of unprepared managers.

Bring *Managing the Union* Shop training to your managers. Consistently rated "outstanding" by participants who learn:

- **The cardinal rule**: Don't compromise the compromise!
- How to deal with **past practice**
- The 7 tests of **just cause**, the **best grievance defenses** and how to write **strong reprimands**
- The 6 steps to a **winning grievance investigation**

There are **2 options** to provide *Managing the Union* Shop training to **your** management team:
- Delivery <u>at your location</u>; or
- Purchase our <u>training kit</u> and conduct the training yourself.

CALL 800-888-9115 to learn more!

More Resources for Unionized Companies

Model Reprimands for the Union Shop
Nearly 100 sample letters of reprimand; document problems and win grievances. $29.99 plus shipping or available on Amazon.

Model Contract Clauses
Over 200 model clauses (strong company and union proposals) plus drafting guide. $39.99 plus shipping or available on Amazon.

How to Investigate Grievances
68-page guide for supervisors. $9.99 plus shipping.

CALL 800-888-9115 to order!

What's Your Next Play?

The Approachability Playbook will take your leadership to the next level.

Buy *The Approachability Playbook*. Grab a copy of *The Playbook*. Visit ALplaybook.com and pick up your own copy of the book. Use the sharing options on that page to tell others how they can receive their own copy of *The Approachability Playbook*.

Download Your Free Tools. On that same page, you can download FREE, ready-to-use templates of all the tools in *The Playbook* (including the *Recognizing Gaps Tool* on page 70).

Take and Share the Quiz. Take the "Good Boss" quiz at ALplaybook.com then ask your co-workers, friends, family... and your boss to take it! You get a custom-tailored report highlighting specific actions you can take to build strong daily approachability habits into your routine.

About the Author

Phillip B. Wilson, Esq. is President and General Counsel of Labor Relations Institute, Inc. He is also the founder of Approachable Leadership. He is a national expert on leadership, labor relations and creating positive workplaces. He is regularly featured in the business media including *Fox Business News, Fast Company, Bloomberg News, HR Magazine,* and *The New York Times.*

Prior to joining LRI, Mr. Wilson represented companies nationwide with the Chicago law firm Wessels & Pautsch, P.C. Mr. Wilson represented management exclusively in all areas of labor and employment law, including union representation matters, collective bargaining negotiations, arbitrations and decertifications. Mr. Wilson's experience also includes employment as a Director of Human Resources for a $65 million annual revenue gaming corporation employing over 1,200 people. There he was responsible for all employment, benefits, labor and risk management matters.

Mr. Wilson received his Juris Doctor degree from the University of Michigan Law School. Mr. Wilson completed his undergraduate degree *magna cum laude*, Phi Beta Kappa, from Augustana College.

Phil is the author of multiple books and publications. In addition to *The Approachability Playbook*, he authored *Left of Boom: Putting Proactive Engagement to Work* (which reached #2 on Amazon's Hot HR Books list). Other books and publications include: *The Next 52 Weeks, Managing the Union Shop, Model Contract Clauses*, among many others. He has also written numerous articles and chapters relating to a broad range of workplace issues, including a chapter in the American Bar Association's treatise on The Fair Labor Standards Act.

Mr. Wilson was invited to testify before Congress numerous times on union financial reporting and labor law reform. Mr. Wilson is admitted to the Illinois Bar and is a member of the American Bar Association, the Society of Human Resource Management, US Chamber of Commerce Labor Relations Committee, the Industrial Relations Research Association and other professional organizations. He is also on the Board of Entrepreneur's Organization.

Wilson is a highly regarded speaker, trainer, and an adjunct professor. Phil delivers keynotes, workshops and webinars regularly for conferences, industry groups, and companies across North America and Canada.

About Labor Relations Institute, Inc.

Labor Relations Institute, Inc. is a full-service labor relations consulting firm. Dedicated to the operational freedom, workplace tranquility and profitability of our clients, we help them respond swiftly and effectively to interventions by unions, government agencies and the legal system.

Made in the USA
Coppell, TX
06 March 2026

73133732R00049